W9-AGU-910

AN AUTOBIOGRAPHICAL SKETCH BY JOHN MARSHALL

AN AUTOBIOGRAPHICAL SKETCH BY JOHN MARSHALL

EDITED BY JOHN STOKES ADAMS

DA CAPO PRESS · NEW YORK · 1973

WINGATE COLLEGE LIBRARY
WINGATE, N. C.

Library of Congress Cataloging in Publication Data

Marshall, John, 1755-1835.
  An autobiographical sketch by John Marshall.

  Reprint of the 1937 ed.
  1. Marshall, John, 1755-1835. 2. Story, Joseph,
1779-1845.
E302.6.M4A32   1973   347′.73′2634 [B]   71-160849
ISBN 0-306-70216-9

This Da Capo Press edition of
An Autobiographical Sketch by John Marshall
is an unabridged republication of the first edition published in
Ann Arbor, Michigan, in 1937.

Copyright, 1937, by the University of Michigan

Published by Da Capo Press, Inc.
A Subsidiary of Plenum Publishing Corporation
227 West 17th Street, New York, New York 10011

All Rights Reserved

Manufactured in the United States of America

An Autobiographical Sketch
by John Marshall

61133

John Marshall

From the Statue on the Capitol Grounds by William Wetmore Story

An
Autobiographical Sketch
by John Marshall

Written at the Request of Joseph Story and Now Printed for the First Time from the Original Manuscript Preserved at the William L. Clements Library, Together with a Letter from Chief Justice Marshall to Justice Story Relating Thereto.

EDITED BY JOHN STOKES ADAMS

The University of Michigan Press

Ann Arbor : 1937

COPYRIGHT, 1937
BY THE UNIVERSITY OF MICHIGAN

PRINTED AT THE LAKESIDE PRESS, R. R. DONNELLEY & SONS COMPANY, CHICAGO

Contents

v

Mushrooms

Illustrations

Introduction

Introduction

THE student of history must perforce devote some of his effort to brushing aside the web of legend which the popular mind has woven about the memory of those who have become great in the political history of our country. The importance of the judicial performances of John Marshall has cast a shadow over the story of his early years; his name has become identified with an idea, perhaps with a cause; and Marshall the man seems destined to fill a niche in the gallery of the legendary heroes of the American political scene. Hence any discovery which will increase, however slightly, our knowledge of the man and of his character must be welcomed by the historian and should be equally welcomed by the casual reader.

He who reads Beveridge's monumental *The Life of John Marshall* with the expectation of learning something of the personal details of the life of that great man must be impressed by two things. But a small part of this voluminous work is devoted to his biography, the greater part being given over to the political history of the times. And when one comes to examine the material of its thorough documentation he finds that amazingly few of the sources are traceable to the hand of Marshall himself. He clearly did not have the habit of preserving papers, for nowhere is to be found any distinguished collection of Marshall manuscripts.

In 1818 Joseph Delaplaine, of Philadelphia, who was engaged in issuing a serial publication entitled *Repository of the Lives and Portraits of Distinguished American Characters*, requested Marshall to sit for a portrait and to furnish some account of his "birth, parentage, etc." Accordingly Marshall, who was then in Richmond, wrote Delaplaine a letter dated March 22, 1818, which contained some account of his family and a brief review of his life up to 1801. Before he could use this material Delaplaine discontinued the *Repository*, but this letter under the title "Autobiography of John Marshall" was published in 1848 at Columbus, Ohio, in a pamphlet which also contained Marshall's famous speech in Congress on the case of Jonathan Robbins. It was also published in facsimile in 1852 in *American Historical and Literary Curi-*

osities, edited by John Jay Smith and John Fanning Watson. The Columbus pamphlet was used and quoted in extenso by Justice Horace Gray in the address delivered by him before the Virginia State Bar Association and the Richmond City Bar Association on February 4, 1901.[1] Beveridge made complete use of this letter, as published by Smith and Watson, and cited it in his footnotes as "Autobiography." It has been impossible to ascertain what has become of the original letter.

It is difficult to think of Marshall as the author of an autobiography. His character was marked by simplicity and modesty, and he had none of that egotism which causes a man to imagine that he benefits mankind by talking about himself. Of this fact he has fortunately left a record. James K. Paulding, while engaged in writing his *Life of Washington*, wrote to Marshall and requested an authentic account of the conference which Marshall and Bushrod Washington held with General Washington at Mount Vernon in 1798 and which resulted in Marshall's becoming a representative in the Congress. He wrote Paulding a letter on April 5, 1835,[2] which contains the

[1] John F. Dillon, *John Marshall, Life, Character and Judicial Services as Portrayed in the Centenary and Memorial Addresses and Proceedings throughout the United States on Marshall Day, 1901*, I, 54–56.
[2] *Lippincott's Magazine*, II (1868), 623–625.

authoritative narrative of that celebrated interview and in the course of which Marshall took occasion to say:

The single difficulty I feel in complying with your request arises from my repugnance to anything which may be construed into an evidence of that paltry vanity which, if I know myself, forms no part of my character. To detail any conversation which might seem to insinuate that General Washington considered my engaging in the political transactions of the United States an object of sufficient consequence to induce him to take an interest in effecting it, may look like boasting that I held a more favorable place in the opinion of that great man than the fact would justify.

Until the manuscript here introduced came to light, the two letters described above constituted everything available to the historian which Marshall himself had written touching his personal history except the Journal which he kept from September 7, 1797, to April 11, 1798, while he was envoy to France. This is one of the principal sources of our knowledge of the transactions between the American envoys and Talleyrand and his agents. What has become of the original is not known. It is not in the Archives of the Department of State, nor in the Division of Manuscripts of the Library of Congress, and diligent search elsewhere has been fruitless. Sometime after his return to America in

June, 1798, Marshall delivered it to the Secretary of State, Timothy Pickering. The latter took a copy of the journal and returned it to Marshall under cover of a letter dated October 19, 1798, and Marshall acknowledged its receipt in a letter to Pickering dated November 12, 1798.[3]

The copy taken by Pickering in manuscript is among his Papers now in the Massachusetts Historical Society. It is cited by Beveridge as "official copy."

In his letter to Story (published herewith) Marshall says, "A journal which I kept exhibits a curious account of transactions at Paris," from which we may infer that he at least thought that either the original or a copy was available in 1827. Story undoubtedly inferred that it was then in Marshall's possession, for in the article in the *North American Review* he writes, "During his absence he kept a journal of his diplomatic transactions, which we presume he still possesses."

These three documents, the letter to Delaplaine, the letter to Paulding and the Paris Journal, constituted all of Marshall's own writing bearing upon his personal history which was known to scholars until the death in 1932 of Mrs. Waldo Story, the widow of Justice Story's grandson.

[3] A letter press copy of the former and the original of the latter are among the Pickering Papers in the Massachusetts Historical Society.

Among the family possessions which were sold was the manuscript which is now published for the first time. It was purchased by Professor Marco F. Liberma of Rome, from whom it was acquired by the William L. Clements Library. It is clear that this manuscript, which came into Joseph Story's possession in 1827, remained in his family for one hundred and five years, having been passed on by him to his son, William W. Story, who in turn passed it on to his son, Waldo Story. It is the most important document written by Marshall about himself. It is fuller and more complete than any other personal thing that came from his pen. It fills sixteen foolscap pages and in form is an undated letter. At its top Story wrote

"Written in 1827. J.S."

In that year Story was writing for the *North American Review* a review of Marshall's *History of the Colonies*[4] which had originally been prefixed as an Introduction to the *Life of Washington* and now had been published as a separate work. Story, evidently thinking that the contemplated review offered an opportunity to present a sketch of the life and public services of the Chief Justice, applied to him for biographical data. There can be little doubt that

[4] John Marshall, *A History of the Colonies planted by the English on the Continent of North America, from their Settlement, to the Commencement of that War, which terminated in their Independence.* Philadelphia: Abraham Small, 1824.

this application was oral, but that it was followed by a letter urging compliance. It is to be regretted that this letter, to which Marshall refers as "your favour of the 14th inst.," cannot be located. It brought forth the manuscript now presented. This was used by Story in three articles:

First, in the review of the *History of the Colonies* which was expanded into an article "Chief Justice Marshall's Public Life and Services" published in the *North American Review* for January, 1828.[5]

Second, in "Memoir of the Hon. John Marshall, LL.D., Chief Justice of the Supreme Court of the United States," published in 1833 in the *National Portrait Gallery* and subsequently in Story's collected writings.[6]

Third, in the "Discourse on John Marshall pronounced on the 15th of October 1835 at the request of the Suffolk Bar," which was published in several legal journals, in *The Miscellaneous Writings of Joseph Story*, edited by his son William W. Story (Boston, 1852), and in Dillon, III, 327–380.

In all of these papers Story made extensive use of Marshall's manuscript which he followed with meticulous fidelity. More than half of it can be traced verbatim in

---

[5] Vol. XXVI (New Series, Vol. XVII), 1–40.

[6] *The Miscellaneous Writings, Literary, Critical, Juridical, and Political, of Joseph Story, LL.D.* (Boston, 1835), pp. 183–200.

parts of one or another of these articles. Indeed, in the third are several avowed quotations cited as extracts from "a letter to a friend." It follows that Story's writings were the most authoritative source on Marshall's life up to the time of his appointment to the bench. They were generally so regarded, although, as will be seen, Beveridge questioned them in several particulars. Upon the first two Horace Binney relied implicitly in the preparation of his famous "Eulogy on John Marshall," delivered September 24, 1835, at Philadelphia.[7]

At the time that Marshall wrote this account of his early life he was seventy-two years old. There is no evidence that he relied on any previous notes or other writings, although he may have had before him a copy of the brief letter to Delaplaine. This however seems unlikely, since he omitted from the letter to Story some facts stated in the former, notably the information as to his ancestry. If therefore, as we conjecture, he wrote from memory, it is not surprising that his narrative contains some minor errors which the careful reader will desire to have called to his attention.

He begins his narrative with "I was born on the 24th of Sept[embe]r 1755 in the county of Fauquier," in words

[7] Dillon, III, 281–326.

identical with those used in the Delaplaine letter. Fauquier County was not established until 1759 and Marshall's birthplace in 1755 was in Prince William County.[8]

His most obvious mistakes are in connection with the regiments in which he served and his rank in the army.[9] He entered the service as first lieutenant in his father's regiment, the 3rd Virginia. In December, 1776, he was promoted to captain-lieutenant and transferred to the 15th Virginia Line and on July 1, 1778, was made captain. On September 14, 1778, he was transferred to the 7th Virginia regiment. This was Colonel Daniel Morgan's regiment, which, prior to that date had been designated as the 11th.[10]

Marshall states that the ratification of the Constitution by the Virginia Convention "was carried in the affirmative by a majority of eight voices."[11] The vote was 89 to 79, or a majority of ten.[12] Marshall probably confused this with the vote on a preliminary resolution which would have postponed ratification pending the reference to the other

---

[8] Albert J. Beveridge, *The Life of John Marshall* (Boston and New York, 1916), I, 7, 51.

[9] See p. 5.

[10] Beveridge, *op. cit.*, I, 79, 91, 138; Francis B. Heitman, Historical Register of Officers of the Continental Army (Washington, 1914), pp. 381, 401.

[11] See p. 11.

[12] Jonathan Elliott, *The Debates in the Several State Conventions on the Adoption of the Federal Constitution* (2nd ed.: Philadelphia, 1861), III, 654.

States for their consideration of proposed amendments. This resolution was lost by a vote of 80 to 88.[13] A some-what similar confusion occurs in the account of the inclusion of the word "wisdom" in the address to Washington by the Legislature of Virginia in 1796.[14] That word was actually excluded.[15]

On the other hand, there are things closely touching the personal life of Marshall as to which it seems more reasonable to place reliance upon his memory than upon the conjecture of the historian. Beveridge was aware that in his "Discourse before the Suffolk Bar," Story was relying on information derived directly from Marshall.[16] Yet he has cast doubt upon that narrative in several particulars.

According to Marshall, he was sent to Mr. Campbell's school when he was fourteen and the following year was placed under the care of the parish pastor.[17] Beveridge reverses these occurrences, deliberately differing from Story and Binney.[18] It is safe to assume that the Chief Justice's memory would play no tricks on such a detail as this. The

[13] *Ibid.*, p. 653.

[14] See p. 20.

[15] Beveridge, *op. cit.*, II, 160–162.

[16] Beveridge, *op. cit.*, II, 160–161.

[17] See p. 4.

[18] Beveridge, *op. cit.*, I, 57.

same comment may be made on his statement that he attended a course "of lectures of Natural philosophy given by Mr. Madison then President of William and Mary College," which Beveridge thinks to be very unlikely.[19]

A curious difference between Marshall and his biographer appears in connection with his election to the legislature in 1789. Beveridge says: "Although the people of Henrico County were more strongly against a powerful National Government than they had been when they sent Marshall to the Constitutional Convention the previous year, they nevertheless elected him."[20] On the other hand Marshall himself tells us that the legislature had passed an act allowing a representative to the city of Richmond, and that "the city was federal." The biographer has exaggerated his hero's popularity, but he evens the score when he comes to relate the familiar story of the election of 1795[21] by adding in a footnote: "While this story seems improbable, no evidence has appeared which throws doubt upon it."[22]

This document adds little to our knowledge of Marshall, but so faithful a chronicler had Story been that it serves chiefly to confirm the authority of what he wrote. The

[19] Beveridge, *op. cit.*, I, 155.
[20] Beveridge, *op. cit.*, II, 54.
[21] See pp. 15–16.
[22] Beveridge, *op. cit.*, II, 130.

searcher of sources, however, finds some reward in this discovery. Throughout the narrative the writer emphasizes his aversion to the life of the politician. Always, in the legislature, in the Congress, in the diplomatic service, in the cabinet, he is filled with a desire to return to the feet of his mistress, the Law. And now, too, we finally have the real story of his appointment to the bench, and, fortunately, the refutation of the error into which Beveridge stumbled that Adams had conferred upon him that honor without previous warning.

With the principal manuscript the Storys have preserved Marshall's letter by which he acknowledged a copy of the article to appear in the *North American Review*. This is interesting, both for its comment on that article and for the light it sheds on Marshall's reaction to the progress of democracy. Fortunately, his original draft of this letter is in existence in the possession of the College of William and Mary. This draft is here reproduced, with the gracious consent of Earl G. Swem, Librarian of that institution. It reveals the painstaking care which Marshall gave to the structure and expression of even so personal a composition as a letter to a friend. On the other hand, it is unfortunate that we do not have the letters from Story to Marshall which evoked the papers here published. The reference to the contents of these letters must, in their absence, remain somewhat obscure.

JOHN STOKES ADAMS

PHILADELPHIA, 1937

The Autobiographical Sketch
by John Marshall

The Autobiographical Sketch[1]

My Dear Sir:

THE events of my life are too unimportant, and have too little interest for any person not of my immediate family, to render them worth communicating or preserving. I felt therefore some difficulty in commencing their detail, since the mere act of detailing, exhibits the appearance of attaching consequence to them; — a difficulty which was not overcome till the receipt of your favour of the 14th inst. If I conquer it[2] now, it is because the request is made by a partial and highly valued friend.

I was born on the 24th of Septr. 1755 in the county of Fauquier at that time one of the frontier counties of Virginia. My Father possessed scarcely any fortune, and had

---

[1] A.L.S.; manuscript in the William L. Clements Library. The original spelling and punctuation are reproduced, with the exception of superior letters.

[2] In the MS "this difficulty" has been crossed out, and "it" interlined.

received a very limited education; — but was a man to whom nature had been bountiful, and who had assiduously improved her gifts. He superintended my education, and gave me an early taste for history and for poetry. At the age of twelve I had transcribed Pope's essay on man, with some of his moral essays.

There being at that time no grammar school in the part of the country in which my Father resided I was sent, at fourteen, about one hundred miles from home, to be placed under the tuition of Mr. Campbell a clergyman of great respectability. I remained with him one year, after which I was brought home and placed under the care of a Scotch gentleman who was just introduced into the parish as Pastor, and who resided in my Fathers family. He remained in the family one year, at the expiration of which time I had commenced reading Horace and Livy. I continued my studies with no other aid than my Dictionary. My Father superintended the English part of my education, and to his care I am indebted for anything valuable which I may have acquired in my youth. He was my only intelligent companion; and was both a watchfull parent and an affectionate instructive friend. The young men within my reach were entirely uncultivated; and the time I passed with them was devoted to hardy athletic exercises.

About the time I entered my eighteenth year, the controversy between Great Britain and her colonies had assumed so serious an aspect as almost to monopolize the attention of the old and the young. I engaged in it with all the zeal and enthusiasm which belonged to my age; and devoted more time to learning the first rudiments of military exercise in an Independent company of the gentlemen of the county, to training a militia company in the neighbourhood, and to the political essays of the day, than to the classics or to Blackstone.

In the summer of 1775 I was appointed a first lieutenant in a company of minute men designed for actual service, who were assembled in Battalion on the first of September. In a few days we were ordered to march into the lower country for the purpose of defending it against a small regular and predatory force commanded by Lord Dunmore. I was engaged in the action at the Great Bridge; and was in Norfolk when it was set on fire by a detachment from the British ships lying in the river, and afterwards when the remaining houses were burnt by orders from the Committee of safety.

In July 1776 I was appointed first Lieutenant in the 11th Virginia regiment on continental establishment; and, in the course of the succeeding winter marched to the north, where, in May 1777, I was promoted to the rank of Captain. I was in the skirmish at iron hill where the Light Infantry was engaged; and in the battles of Brandy Wine, German town, and Monmouth.

As that part of the Virginia line which had not marched to Charleston was dissolving by the expiration of the terms for which the men had enlisted, the officers were directed to return home in the winter of 1779–80, in order to take charge of such men as the legislature should raise for them. I availed myself of this inactive interval for attending a course of law lectures given by Mr. Wythe, and of lectures of Natural philosophy given by Mr. Madison then President of William and Mary College. The vacation commenced in july when I left the university, and obtained a license to practice law. In October I returned to the army, and continued in service until the termination of Arnolds invasion after which, in February 1781, before the invasion of Phillips, there being a redundancy of officers, I resigned my commission. I had formed a strong attachment to the young lady whom I afterwards married; and, as we had more officers than soldiers, thought I might without violating the duty I owed my country, pay some attention to my future prospects in life.

It was my design to go immediately to the bar; but the

invasion of Virginia soon took place, and the courts were closed till the capitulation of Lord Cornwallis. After that event the courts were opened and I commenced practice.

In the spring of 1782 I was elected a member of the legislature; and, in the autumn of the same year was chosen a member of the Executive Council. In January 1783 I was married to Miss Ambler the second daughter of our then Treasurer, and in april 1784 resigned my seat at the Council board in order to return to the bar. In the same month I was again elected a member of the legislature for the county of Fauquier of which I was only a nominal resident having resided actually in Richmond as a member of the Council. Immediately after the election I established myself in Richmond for the purpose of practicing law in the superior courts of Virginia.

My extensive acquaintance in the army was of great service to me. My numerous military friends, who were dispersed over the state, took great interest in my favour, and I was more successful than I had reason to expect. In April 1787, I was elected[3] into the legislature for the county in which Richmond stands; and though devoted to my profession, entered with a good deal of spirit into the politics of the state. The topics of the day were paper

[3] Justice Marshall first wrote "again elected," but crossed out "again."

money, the collection of taxes, the preservation of public faith, and the administration of justice. Parties were nearly equally divided on all these interesting subjects; and the contest concerning them was continually renewed. The state of the Confederacy was also a subject of deep solicitude to our statesmen. Mr. James Madison had been for two or three years a leading member of the House of Delegates, and was the parent of the resolution for appointing members to a general Convention to be held at Philadelphia for the purpose of revising the confederation. The question whether a continuance of the Union or a separation of the states was most to be desired was some times discussed; and either side of the question was supported without reproach. Mr. Madison was the enlightened advocate of Union and of an efficient federal government; but was not a member of the legislature when the plan of the constitution was proposed to the states by the General Convention. It was at first favorably received; but Mr. P. Henry, Mr. G. Mason, and several other gentlemen of great influence were much opposed to it, and permitted no opportunity to escape of inveighing against it and of communicating their prejudices to others. In addition to state jealousy and state pride, which operated powerfully in all the large states, there were some unacknowledged motives

of no inconsiderable influence in Virginia. In the course of
the session, the unceasing efforts of the enemies of the
constitution made a deep impression; and before its close,
a great majority showed a decided hostility to it. I took an
active part in the debates on this question and was uniform
in support of the proposed constitution.

When I recollect the wild and enthusiastic democracy
with which my political opinions of that day were tinctured,
I am disposed to ascribe my devotion to the union, and to
a government competent to its preservation, at least as
much to casual circumstances as to judgement. I had
grown up at a time when a love of[4] union and resistance to
the claims of Great Britain were the inseparable inmates
of the same bosom;—when patriotism and a strong fellow
feeling with our suffering fellow citizens of Boston were
identical;—when the maxim "united we stand, divided
we fall" was the maxim of every orthodox American; and
I had imbibed these sentiments so thoughroughly [*sic*]
that they constituted a part of my being. I carried them
with me into the army where I found myself associated
with brave men from different states who were risking life
and everything valuable in a common cause believed by
all to be most precious; and where I was confirmed in the

4 "A love of" is an interlineation.

habit of considering America as my country, and congress as my government. I partook largely of the sufferings and feelings of the army, and brought with me into civil life an ardent devotion to its interests. My immediate entrance into the state legislature opened to my view the causes which had been chiefly instrumental in augmenting those sufferings, and the general tendency of state politics convinced me that no safe and permanent remedy could be found but in a more efficient and better organized general government. The questions too, which were perpetually recurring in the state legislatures, and which brought annually into doubt principles which I thought most sound, which proved that everything was afloat, and that we had no safe anchorage ground, gave a high value in my estimation to that article in the constitution which imposes restrictions on the states. I was consequently a determined[5] advocate for its adoption, and became a candidate for the convention to which it was to be submitted.

The county in which I resided was decidedly antifederal, but I was at that time popular, and parties had not yet become so bitter as to extinguish the private affections.

A great majority of the people of Virginia was antifederal; but in several of the counties most opposed to the

[5] "Decided" was first written, but cancelled.

adoption of the constitution, individuals of high character and great influence came forward as candidates and were elected from personal motives. After an ardent and eloquent discussion to which justice never has been and never can be done, during which the constitution was adopted by nine states, the question was carried in the affirmative by a majority of eight voices.

I felt that those great principles of public policy which I considered as essential to the general happiness were secured by this measure & I willingly relinquished public life to devote myself to my profession. Indeed the county was so thoroughly antifederal, & parties had become so[6] exasperated, that my election would have been doubtful. This however was not my motive for withdrawing from the legislature. My practice had become very considerable, and I could not spare from its claims on me so much time as would be necessary to maintain such a standing in the legislature as I was desirous of preserving. I was pressed to become a candidate for[7] congress; and, though the district was unequivocally antifederal I could have been elected because that party was almost equally divided between two candidates who were equally obstinate and much embit-

[6] "Entirely" was written at this point, and then stricken out.
[7] "The" was originally written, but stricken out.

tered against each other. The struggle between the ambition of being engaged in the organization of the government, and the conviction of the injury which would be sustained by my private affairs was at length terminated in the victory of prudence, after which the federalists set up and elected Colonel Griffin, who obtained rather more than one third of the votes in the district which constituted a plurality.

Colonel Griffin named me to General Washington as the attorney for the district, an office which I had wished, but I declined accepting it because at that time the circuit courts of the United States were held at two distinct places far apart, and distant from the seat of government where the superior courts of the state sat. Consequently I could not attend them regularly without some detriment to my state practice. Before this inconvenience was removed the office was conferred on another gentleman.

In December 1788 the legislature passed an act allowing a representative to the city of Richmond, and I was almost unanimously invited to become a candidate. The city was federal. I yielded to the general wish partly because a man changes his inclination after retiring from public life, partly because I found the hostility to the government so strong in the legislature as to require from its friends all the support they could give it, and partly because the capitol was then completed, and the courts and the legislature sat in the same building, so that I could without much inconvenience [leave?][8] the bar to take part in any debate in which I felt a particular interest.

I continued in the assembly for the years 1789 & 1790 &[9] 1791, during which time almost every important measure of the government was discussed, and the whole funding system was censured; that part of it especially which assumes the state debts was pronounced unconstitutional. After the session of 1791 I again withdrew from the assembly, determined to bid a final adieu to political life.

The arrival and conduct of Mr. Genet excited great sensation throughout the southern states. We were all strongly attached to France—scarcely any man more strongly than myself. I sincerely believed human liberty to depend in a great measure on the success of the French revolution. My partiality to France however did not so entirely pervert my understanding as to render me insensible to the danger of permitting a foreign minister to mingle himself in the management of our affairs, and to intrude himself

[8] A hole is torn in the page at this point.
[9] "During & I believe" has been crossed out and "&" substituted.

WINGATE COLLEGE LIBRARY
WINGATE, N. C.

between our government and people. In a public meeting of the citizens of Richmond, some of the earliest if not the very first resolutions were passed expressing strong disapprobation of the irregular conduct of Mr. Genet, our decided sense of the danger of foreign influence, and our warm approbation of the proclamation of neutrality. These resolutions, and the address to the President which accompanied them, were drawn and supported by me.

The resentments of the great political party which led Virginia had been directed towards me for some time, but this measure brought it into active operation. I was attacked with great virulence in the papers and was so far honoured in Virginia as to be associated with Alexander Hamilton, at least so far as to be termed his instrument. With equal vivacity I defended myself and the measures of the government. My constant effort was to show that the conduct of our government respecting its foreign relations were such as a just self-respect and a regard for our rights as a sovereign nation rendered indispensable, and that our independence was brought into real danger by the overgrown & inordinate influence of France. The public & frequent altercations in which I was unavoidably engaged gradually weakened my decision never again to go into the legislature, & I was beginning to think of changing my determination on that subject, when the election in the spring of 1795 came on.

From the time of my withdrawing from the legislature two opposing candidates had divided the city, the one was my intimate friend whose sentiments were very much those which I had entertained, and the other was an infuriated politician who thought every resistance of the will of France subserviency to Britain, and an adhesion to the coalition of despots against liberty. Each election between these gentlemen, who were both popular, had been decided by a small majority; & that which was approaching was entirely doubtful. I attended at the polls to give my vote early & return to the court which was then in session at the other end of the town. As soon as the election commenced a gentleman came forward and demanded that a poll should be taken for me. I was a good deal surprized at this entirely unexpected proposition & declared my decided dissent. I said that if my fellow citizens wished it I would become a candidate at the next succeeding election, but that I could not consent to serve this year because my wishes & my honour were engaged for one of the candidates. I then voted for my friend & left the polls for the court which was open and waiting for me. The gentleman said that he had a right to demand a poll for whom he pleased, & persisted in his demand that one should be opened for me—I might if elected refuse to obey the voice of my constituents if I chose to do so. He then gave his vote for me.

As this was entirely unexpected—not even known to my brother who though of the same political opinions with myself[10] was the active & leading partisan of the candidate against whom I had voted, the election was almost suspended for ten or twelve minutes, and a consultation took place among the principal freeholders. They then came in and in the evening information was brought me that I was elected. I regretted this for the sake of my friend. In other respects I was well satisfied at being again in the assembly.

Throughout that part of the year which followed the advice of the senate to ratify Mr. Jays treaty, the whole country was agitated with that question. The commotion began at Boston and seemed to rush through the Union with a rapidity and violence which set[11] human reason and common sense at defiance. The first effort was to deter the President from ratifying the instrument—the next to induce Congress to refuse the necessary appropriations. On this occasion too a meeting of the citizens of Richmond

---

[10] "Though of the same political opinions with myself" is an addition between the lines; so too is "almost" two lines below.

[11] "Seemed to set" was originally written, but corrected by striking out "seemed to."

was convened and I carried a series of resolutions approving the conduct of the President.[12]

As this subject was one in which every man who mingled with public affairs was compelled to take part, I determined to make myself master of it, and for this purpose perused carefully all the resolutions which were passed throughout the United States condemning the treaty and compared them with the instrument itself. Accustomed as I was to political misrepresentation, I could not view without some surprize the numerous gross misrepresentations which were made on this occasion; and the virulent asperity, with which the common terms of decency in which nations express their compacts with each other, was assailed. The constitutionality of the treaty was attacked with peculiar vehemence, and, strange as it may appear, there was scarcely a man in Virginia who did not believe that a commercial treaty was an infringement of the power given to Congress to regulate commerce. Several other articles of the treaty were pronounced unconstitutional; but, on the particular ground of commerce, the objectors believed themselves to be invulnerable.

As it was foreseen that an attempt would be made in the

[12] Justice Marshall first wrote "President, & I carrie——," but crossed out the words after "President" and changed the comma to a period.

legislature to prevent the necessary appropriations, one or two of my cautious friends advised me not to engage in the debate. They said that the part which it was anticipated I would take, would destroy me totally. It was so very unpopular that I should scarcely be permitted to deliver my sentiments, and would perhaps be treated rudely. I answered that the subject would not be introduced by me; but, if it should be brought before the house by others, I should undoubtedly take the part which became an independent member. The subject was introduced; and the constitutional objections were brought forward most triumphantly. There was perhaps never a political question on which any division of opinion took place[13] which was susceptible of more complete demonstration, and I was fully prepared not only on the words of the constitution and the universal practice of nations, but to show on the commercial proposition especially, which was selected by our antagonists as their favorite ground, that Mr. Jefferson, and the whole delegation from Virginia in Congress, as well as all our leading men in the convention on both sides of the question, had manifested unequivocally the opinion that a commercial treaty[14] was constitutional. I had

[13] "Place" is written above "took place," but crossed out.
[14] "Treaty" is written above "question," which has been crossed out.

reason to know that a politician even in times of violent party spirit maintains his respectability by showing his strength; and is most safe when he encounters prejudice most fearlessly. There was scarcely an intelligent man in the house who did not yield his opinion on the constitutional question. The resolution however was carried on the inexpediency of the treaty.[15]

I do not know whether the account given of this debate, which was addressed to some members of Congress in letters from Richmond, and was published, was written by strangers in the gallery or by some of my partial friends. Be this as it may my arguments were spoken of in such extravagant terms as to prepare the federalists of Congress to receive me with marked attention and favour, the ensuing winter when I attended in Philadelphia to argue the cause respecting British debts before the supreme court of the United States. I there became acquainted with Mr. Cabot, Mr. Ames, & Mr. Dexter & Mr. Sedgewic [*sic*],[16] of Massachusetts, with Mr. Wadsworth of Connecticut and with Mr. King of New York. I was delighted with these gentlemen. The particular subject which introduced me to their notice was at that time so interesting, and a

[15] "Inexpediency of the" was repeated, but corrected by striking out the repeated words.

[16] This last name was added later between the lines.

Virginian who supported with any sort of reputation the measures of the government was such a *rara avis*, that I was received by them all with a degree of kindness which I had not anticipated. I was particularly intimate with Ames, & could scarcely gain credit with him when I assured him that the appropriations would be seriously opposed in Congress.

It was about or perhaps a little after[17] this time that I was invited by General Washington to take the office of Attorney General of the United States. I was too deeply engaged in the practice in Virginia to accept this office, though I should certainly have preferred it to any other.

I continued in the assembly though I took no part in the current business. It was I think in the session of 1796–97 that I was engaged in a debate which called forth all the strength and violence of party. Some Federalist moved a resolution expressing the high confidence of the house in the virtue, patriotism, and wisdom of the President of the United States. A motion was made to strike out the word "wisdom." In the debate the whole course of the administration was reviewed, and the whole talent of each party was brought into action. Will it be believed that the word was retained by a very small majority. A very small

[17] "After" is a correction for "before" in the MS.

majority in the legislature of Virginia acknowledged the wisdom of General Washington.

When the cabinet decided on recalling Mr. Monroe from France, the President invited me to succeed him. But I thought my determination to remain at the bar unalterable, and declined the office. My situation at the bar appeared to me to be more independent and not less honorable than any other, and my preference for it was decided.

In June 1797 I was placed by Mr. Adams, then President of the United States, in the commission for accomodating our differences with France, and received a letter requesting my attendance in Philadelphia in order to receive the communications of the government respecting the mission previous to my embarcation. It was the first time in my life that I had ever hesitated concerning the acceptance of office. My resolution concerning my profession had sustained no change. Indeed my circumstances required urgently that I should adhere to this resolution because I had engaged with some others in the purchase of a large estate the arrangements concerning which were not yet made. On the other hand I felt a very deep interest in the state of our controversy with France. I was most anxious and believed the government to be most anxious for the adjustment of our differences with that republic. I felt some confidence in the good dispositions which I should carry with me into the negotiation, and in the temperate firmness with which I should aid in the investigations which would be made. The subject was familiar to me, and had occupied a large portion of my thoughts. I will confess that the *eclat* which would attend a successful termination of the differences between the two countries had no small influence over a mind in which ambition, though subjected to controul, was not absolutely extinguished. But the consideration which decided me was this. The mission was temporary, and could not be of long duration. I should return after a short absence, to my profession, with no diminution of character, &, I trusted, with no diminution of practice. My clients would know immediately that I should soon return & I could make arrangements with the gentlemen of the bar which would prevent my business from suffering in the meantime. I accepted the appointment and repaired to Philadelphia where I embarked for Amsterdam.[18] I found General Pinckney at the Hague, and we obtained passports from the Minister of France at that place to secure our passage[19] in safety to

[18] An interlined correction for "Europe."
[19] Justice Marshall first wrote "to" after "passage," and then crossed it out.

Paris. While at the Hague intelligence was received of that revolution which was effected in the French government by the seizure of two of the Directory and of a majority of the legislature by a military force acting under the orders of three of the Directory combined with a minority of the councils. This revolution blasted every hope of an accomodation between the United States and France.

On reaching Paris General Pinckney and myself communicated our arrival to Mr. Talleyrand & expressed a wish to suspend all negotiation till our colleague should be united with us. In a week or ten days Mr. Gerry joined us, and we immediately addressed ourselves to the minister. The failure of our attempts at negotiation is generally known. A journal which I kept exhibits a curious account of transactions at Paris.[20] As soon as I became perfectly convinced that our efforts at conciliation must prove abortive I proposed that we should address a memorial to Mr. Talleyrand in which we should review fully the reciprocal complaints of the two countries against each other, and bring the whole controversy, at least our view of it before the French government in like manner as if we had been actually accredited. My motive for this was that if the memorial should fail to make its due impression on the

---

[20] This whole sentence is an interlined addition.

government of France, it would show the sincerity with which we had laboured to effect the objects of our mission, and could not fail to bring the controversy fairly before the American People and convince them of the earnestness with which the American government sought a reconciliation with France. General Pinckney concurred with me in sentiment and we acted most cordially together. I found in him a sensible man, and one of high and even romantic honour. Mr. Gerry took a different view of the whole subject. He was unwilling to do anything, and it was with infinite difficulty we prevailed on him to join us in the letter to the minister of exterior relations. It was with the same difficulty we prevailed on him to sign the reply to this answer of the minister.[21] We were impatient to hasten that reply from a fear that we should be ordered[22] to leave France before it could be sent. We knew very well that this order would come and there was a trial of skill between the minister and ourselves, (Genl. Pinckney & myself) he endeavouring to force us to demand our passports, we endeavouring to impose on[23] him the necessity of sending them. At length the passports came and I hastened to Bordeaux to embark for the United States. On my arrival

[21] "Of the minister" is an interlined addition; so also "a" in the third line below.
[22] After "ordered," "out" was first written, but stricken out.
[23] "Impose on" is a correction for "force."

in New York I found the whole country in a state of agitation on the subject of our mission. Our dispatches had been published and their effect on public opinion had fully equalled my anticipations.

I returned to Richmond with a full determination to devote myself entirely to my professional duties, and was not a little delighted to find that my prospects at the bar had sustained no material injury from my absence. My friends welcomed my return with the most flattering reception, and pressed me to become a candidate for Congress. My refusal was peremptory, and I did not believe it possible that my determination could be shaken. I was however mistaken.

General Washington gave a pressing invitation to his nephew, the present Judge, & myself, to pass a few days at Mount Vernon. He urged us both very earnestly to come into Congress & Mr. Washington assented to his wishes. I resisted, on the ground of my situation, & the necessity of attending to my pecuniary affairs. I can never forget the manner in which he treated this objection.

He said there were crises in national affairs which made it the duty of a citizen to forego his private for the public interest. We were then in one of them. He detailed his opinions freely on the nature of our controversy with

France and expressed his conviction that the best interests of our country depended on the character of the ensuing Congress. He concluded a very earnest conversation, one of the most interesting I was ever engaged in, by asking my attention to his situation. He had retired from the Executive department with the firmest determination never again to appear in a public capacity. He had communicated this determination to the public, and his motives for adhering to it were too strong not to be well understood. Yet I saw him pledged to appear once more at the head of the American army. What must be his convictions of duty imposed by the present state of American affairs?

I yielded to his representations & became a candidate. I soon afterwards received a letter from the Secretary of state offering me the seat on the bench of the supreme court which had become vacant by the death of Judge Iredell; but my preference for the bar still continued & I declined it. Our brother Washington was intercepted in his way to Congress by this appointment.

My election was contested with unusual warmth, but I succeeded, and took my seat in the House of Representatives in Decr. 1799. There was a good deal of talent in that Congress both for and against the administration, and I contracted friendships with several gentlemen whom I shall never cease to value. The greater number of them are no more.

In May 1800, as I was about to leave Philadelphia (though Congress was still in session) for the purpose of attending the courts in Richmond, I stepped into the war office in order to make some[24] enquiries respecting patents for some of my military friends, and was a good deal struck with a strange sort of mysterious coldness which I soon observed in the countenance of Mr. McHenry, the secretary of war, with whom I had long been on terms of friendly intimacy. I however prosecuted my enquiries until they brought me into conversation with Mr. Fitzsimmons the chief clerk, who congratulated me on being placed at the head of that department, and expressed the pleasure it gave all those who were engaged in it. I did not understand him, and was really surprized at hearing that I had been nominated to the senate as secretary of war. I did not believe myself to be well qualified for this department, and was not yet willing to abandon my hopes of reinstating myself at the bar. I therefore addressed a letter to Mr. Adams making my acknowledgements for his notice of me, and requesting that he would withdraw my name from the

[24] "In order to make some" was substituted for the originally written "for the purpose of making." In the next line "friends" was interlined.

senate, as I was not willing openly to decline a place in an administration which I was disposed cordially to support. After writing this letter I proceeded immediately to Virginia.

Mr. Adams did not withdraw my name, & I believe the nomination was approved. I had not been long in Virginia when the rupture between Mr. Adams and Mr. Pickering took place, and I was nominated to the senate as secretary of state. I never felt more doubt than on the question of accepting or declining this office. My decided preference was still for the bar. But on becoming a candidate for Congress I was given up as a lawyer, and considered generally as entirely a political man. I lost my business alltogether, and perceived very clearly that I could not recover any portion of it without retiring from Congress. Even then I could not hope to regain the ground I had lost. This experiment however I was willing to make, and would have made had my political enemies been quiet. But the press teemed with so much falsehood, with such continued and irritating abuse of me that I could not bring myself to yield to it. I could not conquer a stubbornness of temper which determines a man to make head against and struggle with injustice. I felt that I must continue a candidate for Congress, and consequently could not replace myself at the bar. On the other hand the office was precisely that which I wished, and for which I had vanity enough to think myself fitted. I should remain in it while the party remained in power; should a revolution take place it would at all events relieve[25] me from the competition for Congress without yielding to my adversaries, and enable me to return once more to the bar in the character of a lawyer having no possible view to politics. I determined to accept the office.

I was very well received by the President, and was on very cordial terms with all the cabinet except Mr. Wolcot [*sic*]. He at first suspected that I was hostile to the two exsecretaries, & to himself, because they were all three supposed to be unfriendly to the President to whom I was truely attached. My conduct[26] soon convinced him however that I had no feeling of that sort, after which I had the satisfaction of finding myself on the same cordial footing with him as with the rest of the cabinet.

On the resignation of Chief Justice Ellsworth I recommended Judge Patteson [*sic*] as his successor. The President objected to him, and assigned as his ground of objection that the feelings of Judge Cushing would be wounded by passing him and selecting a junior member of the

[25] "Remove" has been corrected in the MS to "relieve."
[26] "My conduct" is a correction for "I."

bench. I never heard him assign any other objection to Judge Patteson [*sic*], though it was afterwards suspected by many that he was believed to be connected with the party which opposed the second attempt at negotiation with France. The President himself mentioned Mr. Jay, and he was nominated to the senate. When I waited on the President with Mr. Jays letter declining the appointment he said thoughtfully "Who shall I nominate now"? I replied that I could not tell, as I supposed that his objection to Judge Patteson [*sic*] remained. He said in a decided tone "I shall not nominate him." After a moments hesitation he said "I believe I must nominate you". I had never before heard myself named for the office and had not even[27] thought of it. I was pleased as well as surprized, and bowed in silence. Next day I was nominated, and, although the nomination was suspended by the friends of Judge Patteson [*sic*], it was I believe when taken up[28] unanimously approved. I was unfeignedly gratified at the appointment, and have had much reason to be so. I soon received a very friendly letter from Judge Patteson [*sic*] congratulating me on the occasion and expressing [his][29] hopes that I

[27] "Myself" was first written, and "even" substituted.

[28] "When taken up" is interlined.

[29] A hole is torn in the page at this point. "Occasion," in this line was substituted for "appointment."

On the resignation of Chief Justice Ellsworth
I recommended Judge Patterson as his successor. The President
objected to him, and assigned as his ground of objection that the
feelings of Judge Cushing would be wounded by passing him
and selecting a junior member of the bench. I never heard him
assign any other objection to Judge Patterson, though it was after
wards suspected by many that he was believed to be connected
with the party which opposed the second attempt at negotiation
with France. The President himself mentioned Mr. Jay, and he
was nominated to the senate. When I waited on the President with
Mr. Jays letter declining the appointment he said thoughtfully

who shall I nominate now"? I replied that I could not tell, as I supposed
his objection to Judge Patterson remained. He said in a decided tone "I shall
nominate you". After a moments hesitation he said I believe
I must nominate you". I had never before heard myself named for
the office and had not even thought of it. I was pleased as
well as surprized, and bowed in silence. Next day I was no
minated, and, although the nomination was suspended by the
friends of Judge Patterson, it was I believe, when taken up, unanimously appro
ved. I was unfeignedly gratified at the appointment, and have had
such reason to bless it. I soon received a very friendly letter from Judge Pat
son congratulating me on the occasion and expressing
hopes that I might long retain the office truely grateful for the
cordiality towards me which uniformly marked his conduct.

Facsimile of a portion of the letter from Chief Justice Marshall to Justice Story relating to the appointment to the Supreme Court

might long retain the office.[30] I felt truely grateful for the real cordiality towards me which uniformly marked his conduct.

I have my dear Sir been much more minute and tedious in detail than the occasion required, but you will know how to prune, condense, exclude, and vary. I give you the materials of which you will make some thing or nothing as you please—taking this only with you, that you will be sure to gratify me by pursuing precisely the tract you had marked out for yourself, & admitting nothing which may overload the narrative according to the original plan. Do not insert any thing from the suspicion that I may look for it because I have introduced it into my narrative.

It would seem as if new and perplexing questions on jurisdiction will never be exhausted. That which you mention is one of the strongest possible illustrations, so far as respects the original act, of the necessity in some instances of controuling the letter by the plain spirit of the law. It is impossible that a suit brought by the U.S. can be within the intention of the exception. There is however great difficulty in taking the case out of the letter. The argument you state is very strong and I am much inclined to yield to it. As no private citizen can sue in a district court on a promissory note I am much inclined to restrain

[30] "It," originally written, was made into "the" and "office" added above the line.

the exception to those district courts which have circuit court jurisdiction. But the difficulty is I think removed by the act of the 3d of March 1815 and by the decision of the last term. I speak of that decision however from memory as I have not yet received 12th Wheaton.

Farewell—with the highest respect & esteem

I am yours

J MARSHALL

Draft of Chief Justice Marshall's Letter
to Justice Story, December 30, 1827

Draft of the Letter to Justice Story[1]

RICHMOND Dec. 30th, 1827

MY DEAR SIR

I HAVE received your flattering letter of the and the still more flattering biography which accompanied it. You will not I am persuaded consider me as affecting diffidence when I express a consciousness that your partial friendship has given an importance to the incidents of my life to which they have no just pretensions, mingled with a fear that many may ascribe to me such an excess of vanity as fully to counterbalance any good quality I may be allowed to possess. These fears however do not chill the warm and grateful sentiments with which I receive every mark of your good opinion. The belief that the writer of this sketch views me through a medium which magnifies whatever may be commendable, and diminishes those failings which others may think serious faults, is

[1] A.L.S.; manuscript in the Library of the College of William and Mary.

35

dearer to my heart than any other consideration connected with praise. Mutual esteem and friendship confer reciprocally one of the most choice and exalted pleasures of which the human mind is susceptible.

I congratulate you[2] on the prospect of a more agreeable winter than you have heretofore spent at Washington. I trust accomodations may be found for Mrs. Story at Mrs. Rapines, and that she will by gracing our table shed the humanizing influence of the sex over our not very polished circle. She must however be forewarned that she is not to monopolize you, but must surrender you to us to bear that large portion of our burthens which belongs to you.

When the Review appears I shall not name the author because there is a part of it concerning which I wish to have some conversation with you.[3] It is that which negatives certain qualities which are undoubtedly not much to be admired. I fear that this may be suspectid [*sic*] to affirm that these qualities belong to another. You will readily conceive the effect of such a suspicion. If therefore my friends should inquire, as probably they may,[4] what

[2] Above this is written "When the review appears I" (see next paragraph).

[3] "With you" is added above the line.

[4] Justice Marshall originally wrote, "If therefore I should be asked by my near friends, as probably I may be," and corrected it by deleting and interlining.

artist[5] has drawn this flattering portrait, I shall not name him for the present.

I have received your letter of the 22d of Dec. and am greatly obliged by the examination you have given the subject concerning which I enquired. My mind had a strong leaning in the direction which yours seems to have taken and you confirm the opinion I was previously disposed to adopt.

I participate in[6] [the] serious feelings which you suggest as growing out of the present contest for the Presidency. I begin to doubt whether it will be practicable to elect a chief Magistrate possessing the powers which the Executive of the U. S. ought to possess. I begin to fear that our constitution is not to be so long lived as its real friends have hoped. What may follow sets conjecture at defiance.[7] I shall not live to see and bewail the consequences of these furious passions which are breaking loose upon us.

Yours affectionately

J Marshall

---

[5] "Artist" is added above the line.

[6] These words were added in the margin. The sentence was originally begun with "The serious feelings," and "The" was struck out.

[7] Justice Marshall began to write, "I however shall not" but crossed it out and wrote this sentence between the lines.

Fair Copy of
Chief Justice Marshall's Letter
to Justice Story,
December 30, 1827

The Fair Copy of the Letter
to Justice Story[1]

RICHMOND Decr. 30th 1827

MY DEAR SIR:

I HAVE received your flattering letter and the still more flattering Biography which accompanied it. You will not I am persuaded consider me as affecting diffidence when I express a consciousness that that [*sic*] your friendship has given an importance to the incidents of my life to which they have no just pretensions. This consciousness is mingled with a fear that many may ascribe to me such an excess of vanity as fully to counterbalance any good quality I may be allowed to possess. These fears however do not chill the warm and grateful sentiments with which I receive every mark of your good opinion. The belief that the writer of this sketch views me through a medium which magnifies whatever may deserve commendation, and diminishes those failings which others may

[1] A.L.S.; manuscript in the William L. Clements Library.

41

deem serious faults, is dearer to my heart than any impression which eulogy, were it even deserved, might make on others. Mutual esteem and friendship confer reciprocally on those who feel the sentiment, one of the most exalted pleasures of which the human mind is susceptible.

When the Review appears I shall not name the author, because there is a part of it concerning which I wish to have some conversation with you. It is that which bestows negative praise by declaring the absence of certain qualities which are undoubtedly not very desirable. I fear that this may be suspected to affirm the presence of these same qualities in another work which has produced a good deal of excitement. You will readily conceive the effect of such a suspicion. If therefore any of my particular friends should enquire, as possibly they may, what artist has drawn the portrait so flattering to myself, I shall not name him for the present.

I congratulate you on the prospect of a more agreeable winter than you have heretofore passed at Washington. I trust accomodations may be found for Mrs. Story at Mrs. Rapines, and that she may be tempted by gracing our table to shed the humanizing influence of the sex over a circle which has sometimes felt the want of it. She must however be forewarned that she is not to monopolize you, but must surrender you to us to bear that large portion of our burthens which belongs to you.

I have received your letter of the 22d of December and am greatly obliged by the examination you have given the subject concerning which I enquired. I had hoped that the point was settled in the commercial towns. My mind had a strong leaning in the direction which yours seems to have taken, and you confirm the opinion I was previously disposed to adopt.

I participate in the serious feelings which you suggest as growing out of the present contest for the Presidency. I begin to doubt whether it will be long practicable peaceably to elect a chief Magistrate possessing the powers which the constitution confers on the President of the United States, or such powers as are necessary for the government of this great country with a due regard to its essential interests. I begin to fear that our constitution is not doomed to be so long lived as its real friends have hoped. What may follow sets conjecture at defiance. I shall not live to witness and bewail the consequences of those furious passions which seem to belong to man.

Yours truely & affectionately

J MARSHALL

Index

Index

47

DATE DUE

OCT 15 '88			
GAYLORD			PRINTED IN U.S.A